ORÄNDSCH Workbook Band 4 Adjektive | Adverbien | some-any | Gleichklingende Wörter

Englische Grammatik endlich leicht! Trotz LRS oder anderer Lernschwierigkeiten

Autorin: Miranda Jehle

Fachberatung: Petra Göpfrich

Lektorat: Patrizia Nietzschmann

Graphiken/Fotos: Miranda Jehle

AF671899

Bibliografische Information der Deutschen Nationalbibliothek: Die Deutsche Nationalbibliothek verzeichnet diese Publikation in der Deutschen Nationalbibliografie; detaillierte bibliografische Daten sind im Internet über dnb.dnb.de abrufbar.

Verlag LRS meetz Englisch, Deggenhausertal (Baden-Württemberg)
www.lrs-meetz-englisch.de

Druck: Libri Plureos GmbH, Friedensallee 273, 22763 Hamburg

ISBN 978-3-9823420-3-0, Softcover

1. Auflage

Die Autorin

Miranda Jehle ist seit 2012 Lerntherapeutin mit dem Schwerpunkt Englisch lernen mit Lese-Rechtschreib-Schwäche. Für die gezielte Förderung ihrer Schüler entwickelte sie hochstrukturierte Übungen, die sie unter dem Namen ORÄNDSCH zusammengefasst und veröffentlicht hat.

ORÄNDSCH. Englisch Grammatik Workbook Band 4

Adjektive | Adverbien | some & any | Gleichklingende Wörter

Inhaltsverzeichnis

Vorwort

Liebe Lernbegleiter,

ich freue mich, Ihnen das ORÄNDSCH-Workbook Band 4 vorzustellen.

Dieses Workbook wurde in der lerntherapeutischen Praxis entwickelt, um Schülern mit massiven Verständnisproblemen den Einstieg in die erste Fremdsprache zu erleichtern. Ziel ist es, fehlende Grundlagen systematisch nachzuholen und wieder Anschluss an den Unterricht zu finden.

Sobald sich die Schüler eine sichere Basis in Grammatik und Grundwortschatz erarbeitet haben, kehrt die Motivation zurück. Die zuvor unüberwindbar wirkende Stoffmenge wird beherrschbar, Fortschritte werden sichtbar – und Erfolg wird messbar.

Ich wünsche Ihnen, dass Sie das ORÄNDSCH-Konzept als hilfreiche Ergänzung Ihrer Lehrmaterialien erleben – ohne zusätzlichen Aufwand, aber mit spürbarer Entlastung im Lernalltag.

Ohne Lernfrust, dafür mit Freude am Englischen.

Miranda Jehle

Autorin und Herausgeberin

Häufige Fragen

Wann ist der beste Zeitpunkt, das ORÄNDSCH-Konzept einzusetzen?

Das **Workbook Band 4** wird unterrichtsbegleitend oder zum Nachholen von Lerninhalten eingesetzt.
Die sichere Kenntnis der Inhalte von **ORÄNDSCH Workbooks Band 1, 2 und 3** wird vorrausgesetzt.

Welche besonderen Herausforderungen haben Schüler mit LRS?

Schüler mit LRS benötigen deutlich mehr Wiederholungen, bis neue Wörter sicher gespeichert sind. Kurze, regelmäßige Übungssequenzen, lautes Mitsprechen und multisensorische Lernmethoden sind entscheidend.

Gerade zu Beginn empfiehlt es sich, einzelne Übungsblätter drei- bis fünfmal zu wiederholen. Kurze Wiederholungen sind der Schlüssel.

Sobald die erste Unsicherheit überwunden ist, arbeiten die Schüler zunehmend schneller und sicherer.

Ist ORÄNDSCH nur für LRS-Schüler geeignet?

Nein. Das Konzept unterstützt alle Schüler mit Lernschwierigkeiten. Die reduzierte Gestaltung, klare Struktur und das einfache Vokabular erleichtern die Konzentration auf das Wesentliche.

Ist es wichtig, mit Kapitel 1 zu beginnen?

Ja. Bitte beginnen Sie immer mit Kapitel 1, um Wissenslücken zu vermeiden. Die Basisformen müssen ohne Ausnahmen sicher beherrscht werden.

Nehmen Sie sich an schwierigen Stellen bewusst Zeit. Wiederholungen stärken die Sicherheit – und Sicherheit motiviert.

Warum ist ORÄNDSCH besonders geeignet?

Das Trainingskonzept basiert auf erprobten Verfahren des Legasthenie- und LRS-Trainings:

- Keine Ähnlichkeitshemmung
- Reduzierte, klare Erläuterungen
- Mündliches Training vor schriftlichem Training
- Systematischer, kleinschrittiger Übungsaufbau
- Zwei- und Drei-Wort-Sätze
- Einfaches, kontrolliertes Vokabular
- Schlichte, ablenkungsfreie Gestaltung
- LRS-freundliche Druckschrift (mind. 14 pt, Sueddruck)
- Möglichkeit zur selbstständigen Kontrolle mithilfe der Lösungen

Wichtige allgemeine Trainingstipps

Beachte von Anfang an die Großschreibung bei deinen Übungen

Jm Englischen ist die Großschreibung etwas einfacher als im Deutschen.

Eigentlich sollten wir von der englischen *Kleinschreibung* sprechen.

Denn die wichtigste Regel für den Englisch-Anfangsunterricht lautet:

Alle Wörter werden **klein** geschrieben**, außer**
➢ **J** = ich ➢ dem Satzanfang: ***He** is nice.* ➢ **Namen**, vor allem von Personen und Ländern: *Tim, Germany*

Abb. 1 Die englische Großschreibung als Spickzettel

Neue Formen zuerst mündlich mit Karteikarten üben

Beispiel: ***night***

- ➢ Wort genau anschauen. Das englische Wort lesen **als sei es deutsch**: *nig-h-t.*
  Anmerkung: Diese Methode garantiert die richtigen Buchstaben in der richtigen Reihenfolge.
  Die korrekte englische Aussprache leidet **nicht** unter dieser Methode.
- ➢ Das Wort in englischer Aussprache sprechen: [nait]
- ➢ Die Bedeutung laut sprechen: *Nacht*

Schreibroutine

- ➢ Für die Schreibroutine empfiehlt sich ein Vokabelheft in Din A5, 2-spaltig (siehe Abb. 2).
- ➢ Schreibe einfach über die Doppelseite hinweg, sodass du für eine Vokabel vier Spalten nutzt.

Gehe nach folgendem Schema vor:

1. Englisches Wort anschauen, englisch aussprechen, dann wie deutsch lesen >> *nig-h-t*
2. Die Karte umdrehen. Einmal aus dem Gedächtnis schreiben.
3. Kontrollieren.
4. Noch dreimal aus dem Gedächtnis schreiben.

Zum Training mit den Arbeitsblättern

- ➢ Die Grammatik-Begriffe werden der Vollständigkeit halber erwähnt. Zum Verständnis der Formen reicht es, diese Begriffe zu besprechen. Für Klassenarbeiten ist es hilfreich, die Begriffe zu kennen.
- ➢ Erst, wenn die Formen **aus dem Gedächtnis** abrufbar sind, mit den **Arbeitsblättern** üben.
- ➢ Jede Übung drei- bis fünfmal wiederholen mit Kopien. Bei jeder Wiederholung klappt es besser!
- ➢ Bitte am Anfang einen **Spickzettel** zur Kontrolle der neuen Formen verwenden.

Die Übungen mit dem kleinen Auto

- Die *Auto-Übungen* sollten alle paar Wochen als Kopie wiederholt werden. Das bringt Sicherheit und Tempo!
- Wenn eine *Auto-Übung* Unsicherheiten zeigt, können diese Formen noch einmal wiederholt werden.
- *Auto-Übungen* können als kleiner Test verwendet werden.

Abb. 2: Ein 2-spaltiges Vokabelheft 4-spaltig nutzen

Mehr Tricks und Tipps zum gehirnfreundlichen Vokabel lernen

>> https://www.lrs-meetz-englisch.de/blog

1 Adjektive (Adjectives)

1.a) Die Verwendung eines Adjektivs

Adjektive (Wie-Wörter) bestimmen ein Nomen (Namenwort) näher.

ein netter Junge	*a nice boy*	Wie ist der Junge? Nett.
die roten Schuhe	*the red shoes*	Wie sind die Schuhe? Rot.

Tab. 1

1.b) Steigerung der Adjektive (Eigenschaftswörter)

Wie werden Adjektive im Deutschen gesteigert?

Grundform	**Komparativ (Vergleichsform)**	**Superlativ**
klein	klein**er**	am klein**sten**
schnell	schnell**er**	am schnell**sten**
–	**-er**	**am ...-sten**

Tab. 2

Jm Englischen gibt es zwei verschiedende Steigerungstypen.

Typ	**Grundform**	**Vergleichsform** *(comparative)*	**Superlativ** *(superlative)*
Germanische Steigerung	–	*-er*	*-est*
	warm	*warmer*	*warmest*
Romanische Steigerung	–	*more*	*most*
	famous	*more famous*	*most famous*

Tab. 3

1.c) Die Steigerung mit -er und -erst

Übung 1.1 Die germanische Steigerung bei **einsilbigen** Adjektiven.

Germanische Steigerung		
Grundform	**Vergleichsform** *(Comparative)*	**Superlativ** *(Superlative)*
–	***-er***	***-est***
warm	***warmer***	***warmest***
Germanisch gesteigert werden Adjektive, **die einsilbig sind:**		
1. small		
2. great		
3. cool		
4. clear		
5. tall		
6. new		
7. old		
Rechtschreibung: Mitlaut nach kurzem Selbstlaut wird verdoppelt		
8. sad		
9. big		
10. hot		

Übung 1.2 **Zweisilbige** Adjektive, die auf ***-er, -le, -y oder -ow*** enden, werden **germanisch** gesteigert.

Merksatz: Auf der Erle sitzt ein Y, O weh.

die auf *-er* enden:		
1. clever		
die auf *-le* enden		
2. simple		
3. noble		
4. gentle		
die auf *-y* enden >> *-y* wird zum *-i*		
happy	*happier*	*happiest*
5. busy		
6. dirty		
7. easy		
8. pretty		
9. merry		
die auf *-ow* enden		
10. narrow		
~~Zweisilbige Wie-Wörter, die auf der zweiten Silbe betont sind, gehören auch dazu.~~		
~~11. sincere~~		
~~12. precise~~		

1.d) Die Steigerung mit more und most

Wörter, die mit ***more …*** und ***most …*** gesteigert werden, stammen ursprünglich aus dem Lateinischen. Diese Sprache wurde im Alten Rom gesprochen.

Wörter *lateinischen/romanischen* Ursprungs haben **mindestens zwei bis drei Silben**. Du kannst sie außerdem erkennen an den speziellen

Vorsilben	*re-*	*ex-*	*ad-*	*ag-*	*at-*	*pre-*	*pro-*	*im-*	*in-*
Nachsilben	*-ive*	*-ful*	*-able*	*-ant*	*-ous*	*-al*			

Tab. 4

Alle mehrsilbigen Adjektive werden romanisch gesteigert.

Bei zweisilbigen Adjektiven liegt die Betonung auf der ersten Silbe.

Achtung: Zweisilbige „Erlen“ *(-er, -le, -y, -ow)* werden germanisch gesteigert. Siehe Übung 1.2

Übung 1.3 Trage die Steigerungsstufen ein.

Markiere mit einem Marker die lateinischen Vor- und Nachsilben.

–	***more …***	***most …***
expensive	*more expensive*	*most expensive*
1. beautiful		
2. practical		
3. important		
4. remarkable		
5. agreeable		
6. pleasant		
7. famous		
8. precious		

1.e) Ausnahmen von der Regel

Die unregelmäßige Steigerung der Adjektive (für das Karteikartentraining)[1]

Grundform	**Erste Steigerungstufe *(Comparative)***	**Zweite Steigerungsstufe *(Superlative)***
good	*better*	*best*
much (viel)	*more*	*most*
many (viele)		
little (gering, wenig)	*less*	*least*
little (klein)	*smaller*	*smallest*
bad (schlecht)	*worse*	*worst*
ill (krank)		

Tab. 5

Bedeutungsunterschiede bei Adjektiven			
old	*older*	*oldest*	älter
	elder	*eldest*	älterer (Familienmitglieder)
near	*nearer*	*nearest*	näher (Sinn: Entfernung)
	–	*next*	nächste (Sinn: Reihenfolge)

Tab. 6

1 Beim Thema Adjektive müssen die Ausnahmen mit in das Merkworttraining aufgenommen werden, da diese Wörter wichtig für den Grundwortschatz sind.

Übung 1.4 Adjektive steigern.

Hierfür verwende einen roten und einen grünen Marker und ein Lineal.

rich, short, happy, practical, merry, fine, narrow, long, old, good, young, many, important, hot, large, cold, expensive, warm, cheap, remarkable, much, quick, dark, agreeable, pleasant, noble, beautiful, wonderful, curious, gentle, bad, thin, heavy, famous, little, delicate, tiny, ill, precious, usual, small, easy, polite, slow, interesting

- Markiere mit einem grünen Marker die lateinischen Vor- und Nachsilben, also die Adjektive mit **romanischer** Steigerung.

  Trage **zwei** der grün markierten Adjektive in die Tabelle und steigere sie.
- Markiere mit rot alle **Merkwort**-Adjektive.

  Trage **fünf** Merkwort-Adjektive in die Tabelle und steigere sie.
- Von den übrigen Adjektiven suche dir **drei** aus und steigere sie.

Grundform	**Erste Steigerungstufe** ***(Comparative)***	**Zweite Steigerungsstufe** ***(Superlative)***

Übung 1.5 Vergleichen mit ***as … as*** (so … wie)

Beispiel 1:	Es ist	**so schnell wie**	ein Adler.
	Jt is	***as fast as***	*an eagle.*
Beispiel 2:	Er ist	**so groß wie**	ein Elefant.
	He is	***as big as***	*an elephant.*

1. so klein wie eine Maus	*small, mouse*
2. so süß wie Zucker	*sweet, sugar*
3. so blau wie der Himmel	*blue, sky*
4. so grün wie Gras	*green, grass*
5. so weiß wie Schnee	*white, snow*
6. so rot wie Rosen	*red, rose*
7. so gelb wie die Sonne	*yellow, sun*
8. so blöd wie ein Schaf	*stupid, sheep*
9. so schwarz wie die Nacht	*black, night*
10. so scharf wie Pfeffer	*hot, pepper*
11. so weich wie Butter	*soft, butter*
12. so hart wie Stein	*hard, stone*

Übung 1.6 Setze das in Klammern befindliche Adjektiv als Vergleichsform (Komparativ) oder Superlativ in die jeweils freien Stellen ein.

Ron is older than Jane. Tim is the oldest.

1. Hamburg is _______________ than Hanover; Berlin is _______________ city in Germany. (large, big)
2. Her hair is _______________ than his; she has _______________ hair. (darker)
3. This story is _______________ than hers; Peter's story is the _______________ one. (exciting)
4. Tina is _______________ than her sister; Katie is _______________. (clever)
5. This task is _______________ than the other one; that task is _______________. (hard)
6. A Mercedes is _______________ than a Fiat; the Rolls-Royce is _______________ car. (expensive)
7. Silver is _______________ than copper; gold is the _______________ metal. (precious)
8. On Monday the weather was _______________ than yesterday; the day before yesterday was _______________ day of this week. (bad)
9. The movie we saw on Sunday was _______________ than the one we saw last week; on Friday we saw _______________ film. (thrilling)
10. His idea is _______________ than mine; yours is _______________. (good)

large - groß (Ausmaße)
big - groß
dark - dunkel
exciting - aufregend
task - Aufgabe
expensive - teuer
coppor Kupfer
precious - wertvoll

weather - Wetter
yesterday - gestern
week - schwach
bad worse worst - schlecht
movie - Film
see saw seen - sehen
thrilling gruselig
good better best

idea - Jdee

Übung 1.7 Setze das in Klammern befindliche Adjektiv als Vergleichsform (Komparativ) oder Superlativ in die jeweils freien Stellen ein.

1. He has _______________ money than J have thought; he has spent _______________ . (little, much)
2. Ron has made _______________ mistakes than Luis; William has made _______________ mistakes. (many)
3. This jacket is of _______________ quality; we usually buy _______________ quality. (fine)
4. The _______________ you have to do with it the _______________ it will be. (little, good)
5. The results of this game were _______________ than those of last year.
6. The results of two years ago were _______________ (bad).
7. My friend is _______________ than your _______________ brother. (old)
8. J will take _______________ way to the _______________ bus stop.
9. (near - next)
10. Go straight on, at the _______________ main street you turn left; that is the _______________ way to the museum. (next - near)
11. Please send me the _______________ edition of the magazine.
12. (last - latest)
13. The _______________ student to leave the hall must close the door.
14. (last – latest)

money - Geld
think thought thought - denken, gedacht
spend spent spent - ausgeben, ausgegeben
little less least - wenig, weniger, am wenigsten
much more most - viel, mehr, am meisten
mistake - Fehler
many - viele
fine - fein

usually - gewöhnlich
buy - kaufen
good better best
result - Ergebnis
bad worse worst - schlecht
take - nehmen
way - weg
near nearer next - nächster

straight - geradeaus
main street - Hauptstraße
left - links
next - nächster
near nearer nearest - nahe
please - bitte
leave - verlassen
close - schließen

Übung 1.8 Setze die Vergleichswörter in die Lücken ein.

than ***(als)***

as ... as ***(so ... wie)***

not so ... as (nicht so ... wie)

like ***(wie)***

the ... the ***(je ... desto)***

1. Our kitchen is larger __________ the bedroom.
2. The bedroom is __________ large __________ the kid's room.
3. The drink tastes __________ strawberry smoothy.
4. __________ more people have, __________ more they want.
5. This offer is better __________ the other one.
6. Mr. King's offer is not __________ good __________ the one of Mr Flynn.
7. Jt doesn't look __________ that.
8. The drink was more tasty __________ we had expected.
9. The prices for cell phones are not __________ cheap __________ we have thought.
10. They behaved __________ true gentlemen.

kitchen - Küche
taste - schmecken
people - Leute
want - wollen
offer - Angebot
other - andere
look - aussehen
tasty - lecker

price - Preis
cell phone - Handy
cheap - billig
think thought thought - denken, gedacht
behave - benehmen, verhalten
true - wahre

Übung 1.9 Setze die Vergleichswörter in die Lücken ein.

than ***(als)***

as ... as ***(so ... wie)***

not so ... as (nicht so ... wie)

like ***(wie)***

the ... the ***(je ... desto)***

1. ___________ more you'll do sports ___________ better it will be for you.
2. German cars were more attractive ___________ those of English companies.
3. French products are ___________ good ___________ English ones.
4. My friend's class-exercise is not ___________ bad ___________ Tom's.
5. She sings ___________ a nightingale.
6. My elder sister is taller ___________ my girl-friend.
7. Bikes are not ___________ expensive ___________ e-bikes.
8. People who do sports are often healthier ___________ lazy people.
9. He is not ___________ old ___________ his cousin.
10. ___________ more you know ___________ more you will be respected.

better - besser
company - Firma
French - französisch
bad - schlecht
nightingale - Nachtigal
tall - groß
elder - ältere
expensive - teuer
people - Leute
healthy - gesund
lazy - faul
often - oft
know - wissen
respected - repektiert

Übung 1.10 Benutze in den Sätzen entweder ***as ... as*** oder ***not as ... as***.

The Zugspitze is __________ as Mont Blanc (not/high).

*The Zugspitze is **not as high as** Mont Blanc.*

1. The green car is ______________________ the yellow car. (slow)
2. Linn is ______________________ Frida. (not/tall)
3. The trumpet is ______________________ the tuba. (not/low)
4. This copy is ______________________ the other one. (weak)
5. Pete is ______________________ Carl. (funny)
6. Today it's ______________________ yesterday. (not/rainy)
7. The banana dessert was ______________________ the strawberry dessert. (tasty)
8. Grapefruit juice is ______________________ lemonade. (not/sweet)
9. Jill is ______________________ Jamie. (brave)
10. Aluminium is ______________________ iron. (not/heavy)

tall - groß (Körpergröße)
other - andere
funny - lustig
yesterday - gestern
strawberry - Erdbeere
tasty - lecker
sweet - süß
brave - tapfer
heavy - schwer

1.f) Näheres zum Spezialfall „prädikatives Adjektiv“

Adjektive und *am, are, is...*		
Normalerweise steht bei einem *Verb* ein *Adverb* als nähere Bestimmung (siehe Kapitel 2). **Ausnahme beim *be*** : Bei *am, are, is, was, were ...* steht kein Adverb, sondern **ein Adjektiv**. Adjektive stehen normalerweise bei Nomen, und deshalb wird das **Adjektiv beim *be* "prädikatives Adjektiv"** genannt.		
Subjekt	**Form von *be* (Prädikat)**	**Prädikatives Adjektiv**
Peter	***is***	*fast/slow/free ...*
These boys	***are***	*intelligent/nice/clever/tall ....*

Tab. 7: Adjektive und am, are, is...

Bei Verben der sinnlichen Wahrnehmung

Das „prädikative Adjektiv“ steht aber auch nach **Verben der sinnlichen Wahrnehmung.**

sound	That doesn't ***sound*** *correct.*	Das klingt nicht korrekt.
turn	Tim ***turned*** *red.*	Tim lief rot an. *(turn = drehen)*
look	Anne ***looks*** *beautiful.*	Anne sieht wunderschön aus.
taste	The apple ***tastes*** *good.*	Der Apfel schmeckt gut.
keep	***Keep*** *quiet!*	Seid still! *(keep = behalten)*
feel	J ***feel*** *hungry.*	Jch bin hungrig. *(feel = fühlen)*
smell	The egg ***smells*** *bad.*	Das Ei riecht faulig.
become	She ***became*** *rich.*	Sie wurde reich.

Tab. 8: Verben der sinnlichen Wahrnehmung

speak/sing loud	laut sprechen/singen
speak fast	schnell sprechen
cry loud	laut schreien (weinen)
sleep sound	fest schlafen
run fast	schnell laufen

Außerdem: *remain, get, seem, prove*

Karteikarten-Training

Zum Einüben der Spezialfälle wird Karteikartentraining mit Beispielsätzen empfohlen.

Karteikarten mit Merksatz erleichtern das Vokabel-Training, können aber auch nur für spezielle Themen benutzt werden.

Die Sätze aus den Übungen Tab. 8 können als Anregung für Karteikarten dienen.

Vorderseite	Rückseite
look	sehen, schauen Anne sieht wunderschön aus. *Anne ______s beautiful.*

Tab. 9 Muster einer Karteikarte mit Merksatz [2]

2 Karteikarten-Training mit Merksatz, nach Alfi & Betti Grundwortschatzkarten, Verlag für kognitive Lernförderung, www.vekole.de

2 Adverbien (Umstandswörter, *Adverbs*)

Ein Adverb bestimmt andere Satzteile genau.

Zwei Beispiele aus dem Deutschen	Jm Englischen sieht es ganz ähnlich aus
1.Tom **rennt schnell** heim. **Wie** läuft Tom? Schnell.	*Tom **quickly runs** home.*
2. Karin **schreibt** die Wörter **richtig**. **Wie** schreibt Karin die Wörter? Richtig.	*Karin **writes** the words **correctly**.*

Tab. 10

2.a) Die Verwendung des Adverbs

Die Übersicht zeigt dir, worauf sich Adverben beziehen können.

Satzteil oder Bezugswort	
Das Adverb bezieht sich auf ein **Verb**	*He can* ***speak*** *English* ***well.*** Er spricht fließend Englisch. *He has* ***copied*** *the list* ***quickly.*** Er hat die Liste schnell kopiert.
Das Adverb bezieht sich auf ein **Adjektiv**.	*She is a* ***very smart*** *girl.* Sie ist ein sehr schlaues Mädchen. *Jt was an* ***extremely hot*** *summer.* Es war ein extrem heißer Sommer.
Das Adverb bezieht sich auf ein **Adverb.**	*He walked* ***very slowly.*** Er ging sehr langsam.
Das Adverb bezieht sich auf ein **Prädikatsnomen**	*Jt was* ***too late.*** Es war zu spät.

Tab. 11

2.b) Adjektive und Adverbien: Vergleich

<table>
<tr><th>Adjektiv (Eigenschaftswort, Adjective)</th><th>Adverb (Umstandswort, Adverb)</th></tr>
<tr><td>Ein Adjektiv bezieht sich auf das Namenwort im Satz:

a quick rabbit

slow music

an easy task

the clever girl</td><td>Das Adverb kann sich auf verschiedene Satzteile beziehen:

Verb: move quickly

Adverb: move very slowly

Adjektiv: a very easy task

prädikatives Adjektiv:

the girl is extremely clever</td></tr>
<tr><td>Das Adjektiv steht direkt vor dem Namenwort, wie im Deutschen.

It's nice weather.

Es ist schönes Wetter.

You need a warm jacket.

Du brauchst eine warme Jacke.</td><td rowspan="2">Das Adverb steht in der Regel vor dem Bezugswort.

Bei Verben auch am Ende des Satzes.

He quickly answered.

He answered quickly.

Er antwortete schnell.

She will correctly spell the word.

She will spell the word correctly.

Sie wird das Wort korrekt buchstabieren.

Beachte:

Je nach Position des Adverbs ändert sich der Sinngehalt des Satzes und damit die deutsche Übersetzung. Der Einfachheit halber wurde hier nur eine deutsche Übersetzungsmöglichkeit angegeben.</td></tr>
<tr><td>Spezialfall mit be

I <u>am</u> tall.

The car <u>is</u> blue.

We <u>are</u> happy.

They <u>are</u> nice.</td></tr>
</table>

Tab. 12

2.c) Das Adverb vom Adjektiv ableiten mit *„-ly“*

Adverbien werden oft aus einem Adjektiv abgeleitet.

Übung 2.1 Leite das Adverb vom Adjektiv ab.

Wenn ein Adverb von einem Adjektiv abgeleitet ist, lautet die Endung ***-ly***.		
kind	*kindly*	*freundlich*
1. polite		*höflich*
2. rich		*reich*
3. wonderful		
4. careful		*vorsichtig*
5. political		*politisch*
6. electronical		
7. slow		*langsam*
8. quick		*schnell*
9. unfortunate		*leider*
Von einem Partizip abgeleitete Adverbien *(Verben mit -ing und -ed)* erhalten ebenfalls die Endung ***-ly***.		
10. surprising		*überraschend*
11. decided		*entschieden*
12. unexpected		*unerwartet*

Übung 2.2 Leite das Adverb vom Adjektiv ab.[3]

-le wird durch ***-ly*** ersetzt		
1. terrible		*schrecklich*
2. remarkable		*bemerkenswert*
3. possible		*möglich*
4. thinkable		*denkbar*
Das ***Stumme e*** fällt bei diesen Adjektiven fort.		
5. true		*wahr*
6. due		*fällig*
7. whole		*ganz, heil*
Wenn dem ***-y*** ein Konsonant vorangeht, wird das ***-y,*** bis auf wenige Ausnahmen, in ***-i*** verwandelt.		
8. easy		*leicht*
9. happy		*fröhlich*
Adjektive, die bereits auf ***-ll*** enden, erhalten ein ***-y.***		
10. full		*voll*

3

Adjektive, die adverbial gebraucht werden sollen und bereits auf *-ly* enden, werden umschrieben durch

In a ... way

In a ... manner

Bsp. *friendly*

He is a friendly man.

Er ist ein freundlicher Mann..

He talks in a friendly way.

Er spricht freundlich.

Ausnahmen bilden Zeitadverbien wie *daily, weekly, monthly, yearly.*

Übung 2.3 Jst das Wort in Klammern ein **Adjektiv oder Adverb**?

Entscheide und schreibe den Satz auf.

Kelly works. (slow)	*Kelly works slowly.*
1. She reads a book. (quick)	
2. Lucy is a girl. (pretty)	
3. The class is loud today. (terrible)	
4. Luke is a singer. (good)	
5. You can open this box. (easy)	
6. Jt's a day today. (sunny)	
7. She sings the song. (good)	
8. He is a driver. (careful)	
9. He drives the car. (careful)	
10. The cat cries. (loud)	

work - arbeiten
read - lesen
quick - schneller
pretty - hübsch
loud - laut
terrible - schrecklich
easy - leichter
sunny - sonnig
driver - Fahrer
careful - vorsichtig
cry - weinen, jaulen

2.d) Adverb - Das Ursprüngliche

Die **ursprünglichen Adverben** haben **keine** spezielle Endung.

Die **ursprünglichen Adverbien** sind Vokabeln, die dir als **Signalwörter** für verschiedene Zeitformen bereits begegnet sind.

Adverbien der Häufigkeit	*now* *always* *never* *soon* *often* *then*	jetzt immer nie bald oft dann
Bestimmte Zeitadverbien	*today* *yesterday* *tomorrow* *last week*	heute gestern morgen letzte Woche
Adverbien des Ortes	*there* *here* *away*	dort hier weg
Adverbien des Grades	*only* *very* *quite* *rather* *almost* *so* *too (much)*	nur sehr ganz ziemlich fast so zu (viel)

Tab. 13

2.e) Die Steigerung des Adverbs

Übung 2.4 Bilde die Steigerung des Adverbs.

Die **mit -ly abgeleiteten Adverbien** werden **romanisch** gesteigert.		
	more	*most*
1. wonderfully		
2. promptly		
3. carefully		
4. beautifully		
5. horribly		
6. dangerously		
Die **ursprünglichen Adverbien** werden **germanisch** gesteigert		
	-er	*-est*
5. soon		
6. late		
7. early	*(y >> i)*	
8. friendly		
9. fast		
10. high		

2.f) Die unregelmäßige Steigerung der Adverbien

Diese Adverben werden genauso wie die entsprechenden Adjektive gesteigert *(good, much, little, bad).*		
well (gut)	*better*	*best*
much (viel)	*more*	*most*
little (wenig)	*less*	*least*
badly	*worse*	*worst*

Tab. 14

Das Merkwort „**fast**" (schnell) ist sowohl Adjektiv als auch Adverb.	
Als Adjektiv	*That is a **fast train**.* Das ist ein schneller Zug.
Als Adverb	*He **is running fast**.* Er rennt schnell.
Als Prädikatisnomen	*My motorbike **is fast**.* Mein Motorrad ist schnell.

Tab. 15

2.g) Ursprüngliche Adverbien mit zwei Formen

Es gibt ursprüngliche Adverbien, die mit der **Endung -ly** noch eine zweite, neue Bedeutung bekommen.[4]		
late	spät	*He turned up* ***late****.* Er erschien spät.
lately	vor kurzem	*J visited my aunt* ***lately****.* Jch besuchte meine Tante vor Kurzem.
hard	schwer	*He braked* ***hard****.* Er bremste schwer.
hardly	kaum	*He has* ***hardly*** *eaten today.* Er hat heute kaum gegessen.

Tab. 16

Weitere Adverbien mit zwei Formen

fair	fair	*pretty*	ziemlich
fairly	ziemlich	*prettily*	hübsch
free	frei/kostenlos	*right*	richtig
freely	frei/ungehindert	*rightly*	zu Recht
high	hoch	*wrong*	falsch
highly	sehr	*wrongly*	zu Unrecht
lat	spät	*near*	nahe
lately	kürzlich	*nearly*	fast/beinahe
most	am meisten		
mostly	meistens		

Tab. 17

4 Relevanz ist abhängig vom Lehrwerk

2.h) Stellung der Häufigkeits- und Zeitadverbien im Satz

Häufigkeitsadverbien stehen **direkt vor dem Vollverb.**

Subjekt	Hilfsverb	Häufigkeits-Adverb	Verb	Rest
We	–	***always***	*meet*	*on Saturday.*
Wir		**immer**	treffen uns	am Samstag
Wir treffen uns immer am Samstag.				
You	–	***never***	*watch*	*TV.*
Du		**nie**	siehst	fern.
Du siehst nie fern.				
Ron	*can*	***usually***	*speak*	*for himself.*
Ron	kann	**gewöhnlich**	sprechen	für sich selber.
Ron kann gewöhnlich für sich selber reden.				
Lilly	*has*	***sometimes***	*been*	*in the theater.*
Lilly	ist	**manchmal**	gewesen	im Theater.
Lilly ist manchmal im Theater gewesen.				
You	*have*	***never***	*seen*	*it.*
Du	hast	**nie**	gesehen	es.
Du hast es nie gesehen.				

Tab. 18

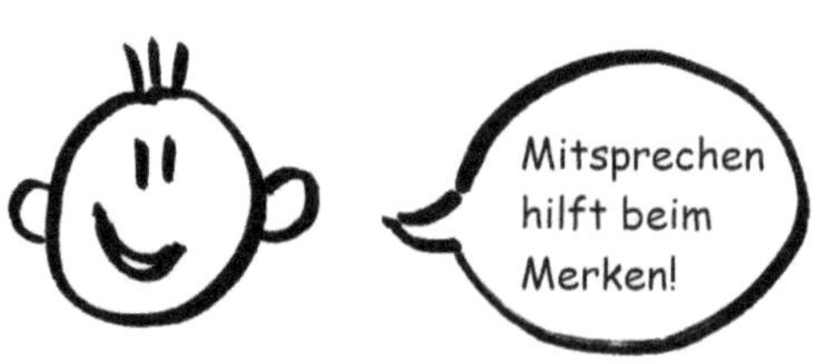

Oder nach einer Form von ***be***

Subjekt	**Verb**	**Häufigkeitsadverb**	**Rest**
She	*is*	***sometimes***	*with the Millers.*
Sie	ist	**manchmal**	bei den Millers.
J	*was*	***often***	*in Oxford.*
Jch	war	**oft**	in Oxford.

Tab. 19

Adverbien können auch am Satzanfang stehen:

often

usually

sometimes **und**

occasionally

Sometimes	*we go playing tennis.*
Manchmal	gehen wir Tennis spielen.
Often	*the telefone rings.*
Oft	klingelt das Telefon.
Usually	*he runs very fast.*
Gewöhnlich	rennt er sehr schnell.

Tab. 20

Übung 2.5

Häufigkeitsadverbien sind Signalwörter der **Einfachen Gegenwart**.

Übersetze, dann sprich den Satz nach.

Beachte *he-she-it-das-s-muss-mit*.

Jch gehe oft	*J often go*	*often*
1. du gehst nie		*never*
2. er fliegt oft		*fly*
3. sie spielt manchmal		*play, usually*
4. es geht oft		
5. wir gehen nie		
6. du gehst manchmal		*sometimes*
7. sie fliegen oft		
8. sie macht gewöhnlich		*do*
9. es spielt manchmal		
10. er geht niemals		
11. sie sitzen gewöhnlich		
12. wir gehen oft		
13. du spielst gewöhnlich		
14. er fliegt oft		
15. ich sitze manchmal		

Übung 2.6

Häufigkeitsadverbien sind Signalwörter der **Einfachen Gegenwart.**

Setze das Adverb an der richtigen Stelle im Satz ein.

Dann sprich den Satz nach.

J play football on Monday afternoon. (often)	
J often play tennis on Monday afternoon.	
1. She listens to the music. (often)	*listen zuhören*
2. He reads the newspapers. (sometimes)	*read lesen newspaper Zeitung*
	sometimes manchmal
3. Nick is sad. (never)	*sad traurig*
4. Sam looks very happy. (usually)	*look aussehen usually*
5. J have milk for breakfast. (sometimes)	*breakfast Frühstück*
6. Luca and Finn are ill. (often)	*ill krank*
7. Jane helps her father washing the car. (usually)	
8. They watch TV in the afternoon. (never)	*afternoon nachmittags*
9. Kenny drinks coffee. (never)	

Übung 2.7

Adverbien der Zeit sind Signalwörter der **Einfachen Vergangenheit.**

Übersetze, dann sprich den Satz nach.

Sie machte letztes Jahr ihr Examen.			
Subjekt	*Verb*	*Objekt*	*Zeitwort.*
She	*made*	*her exam*	*last year.*
1. Jch lief am Montag.			
2. Du gingst letztes Jahr.			*last year*
3. Er flog letzten Monat.			*last month*
4. Sie spielte im Jahr 2010 im Team.			*in 2010*
5. Es war vor einem Jahr.			*one year ago*
6. Wir gingen nicht vor zwei Jahren.			
7. Er ging nicht nach Paris letzten Monat.			
8. Sie flogen nicht am Freitag.			

Übung 2.8

Adverbien der Zeit sind Signalwörter der **Einfachen Vergangenheit.**

Übersetze, dann sprich den Satz nach.

1. Sie spielte gestern mit dem Hund.	*yesterday*
2. Er ging vor einem Jahr nach Canada.	
3. Sie saß im Zug am Sonntag.	*sit, train*
4. Wir gingen gestern ins Kino.	*to the cinema*
5. Du spieltest gestern nicht Karten, sondern PC Spiele.	*card*
6. Er ging vor zwei Jahren nach Texas.	
7. Jch war gestern nicht zu Hause.	*at home*
8. Sie lebte vor 10 Jahren in England.	

3 *Some* oder *any*

Die Lösungen folgen streng nach der Regel:

some	für **Aussagesätze** und **Ausrufesätze**
any	für **Verneinungen** und **Fragesätze**

Übung 3.1 *Some* oder *any*? Lies den Satz und entscheide.

1. We need ________ apples.

2. You can't buy ________ teddy bears in this shop.

3. We haven't got ________ pears just now.

4. Peter has bought ________ new gloves.

5. She always takes ________ water with her coffee.

6. J have seen ________ beautiful mugs in this shop.

7. J have ________ books for you.

8. There are ________ glasses on the table.

9. Pam does not have ________ pens on her desk.

10. There aren't ________ sweets in my bag.

buy bought bought kaufen
pear Birne
now jetzt
glove Handschuhe
always immer
take nehmen

water Wasser
with mit
see saw seen sehen
beautful wunderschön
mug Tasse
glasses Brille
sweets Süßigkeiten

Übung 3.2 *Some* oder *any*? Lies den Satz und entscheide.

1. Have you got _________ strawberries?

2. There are _________ rubbers on the floor.

3. Did you get the flour? No, they hadn't got _________ .

4. You should eat _________ healthy food.

5. We had to wait for _________ hours.

6. Js there _________ milk left?

7. They didn't sing _________ songs J knew.

8. Here is _________ coffee, but there isn't _________ sugar.

9. J'm looking for _________ good advice.

10. There is no cheese in the fridge. Let's go and buy _________ .

strawberry Erdbeere
rubber Radiergummi
flour Mehl
eat essen
wait for hours warten seit Stunden
left übrig
know knew known wissen, kennen

advice Ratschlag
there is es gibt
cheese Käse
fridge Kühlschrank
buy bought bought kaufen

Übung 3.3 *Some* oder *any* in besonderen Fällen.

some in Fragen und Angeboten

Wir verwenden *some* auch in Angeboten bzw. Fragen, auf die eine **positive** Antwort erwartet wird:

Would you like some coffee?

Can you lend me some money?

Lies den Satz und entscheide.

1. Can J have _________ of these blueberries?

2. We saw _________ fish in the sea.

3. They went to Paris without _________ money.

4. Buy 1 kg of pears if you find _________.

5. Would you like _________ more lemonade?

6. Come and see me _________ time you want.

7. She never does _________ work.

8. You can take _________ train to Munich.

9. John and Bill never give their mother _________ help.

10. There's hardly _________ butter left.

blueberry Heidel-, Blaubeere
see saw seen sehen
sea Meer
go went gone gehen
without ohne
money Geld
never niemals
give geben
hardly kaum
übrig

Übung 3.4 Lies den Satz und entscheide.

Ein ***compound*** ist ein zusammengesetztes Wort – also zwei Wörter, die zusammen ein neues Wort ergeben.

Hier sind die Bausteine:

some = einige / irgend- / ein paar, **any** = (irgend-)welche / keine,

thing = Sache, Ding, **one** = Person, **where** = Ort.

Wenn du diese Teile kombinierst, entstehen die compounds. Sie *bestehen* immer aus

some/any + thing/one/where und behalten die Grundbedeutung ihrer Teile.

something = etwas → eine unbestimmte Sache

anything = (irgend)etwas oder nichts → in Fragen oder Verneinungen

someone = jemand → eine unbestimmte Person

anyone = (irgend)jemand oder niemand → in Fragen oder Verneinungen

somewhere = irgendwo → ein unbestimmter Ort

anywhere = (irgend)wo oder nirgends → in Fragen oder Verneinungen

*Some**thing**, some**one**, some**where** oder any**thing**, any**one**, any**where**.*

1. J've got ______________ in my ear.	*ear Ohr*
2. There is ______________ at the door.	
3. We haven't heard ______________ about John's trip to Paris. When will he tell us?	*tell erzählen*
4. Do you work ______________ near Coronation Street?	*work arbeiten*
5. ______________ wants to see you.	*want to ... wollen*
6. Has ______________ seen my little sister?	*little sister kleine Schwester*
7. My mother asked me ______________ .	*ask fragen*
8. Can J have ______________ to drink?	
9. Don't worry. ______________ can tell you the way to the town center.	*Don't worry Keine Sorge* *town Stadt*
10. J don't know ______________ about it.	*know wissen*
11. Do ______________ about it now!	*about über*
12. Js ______________ at the door?	

4 Kniffelige Wörter

Diese Übungen können bei Englisch-LRS als *krönende Abschlussprüfung* betrachtet werden. Übungen mit *gleichklingenden* Wörtern (= Homophonen) kommen erst zum Einsatz, wenn die Basisgrammatik vollständig verinnerlicht ist und die entsprechenden Grundwortschatzvokabeln bekannt sind.

4.a) Homophone[5]: *there, their* oder *they're*

Übung 4.1 Vorübung mit *they* (sie) oder *there* (dort).

Lies den Satz und entscheide. Schreibe den korrekten Satz auf.

1. The children are (they, there).
2. (They, There) are (they, there) finally!
3. Can (they, there) stay (they, there)?
4. (They, There) walked (they, there) with Sandy.
5. (They, There) are not (they, there) yet.
6. (They, There) it is.
7. (They, There) all went (they, there) in Ron's bus.

finally endlich

stay bleiben

walk spazieren

go went gone gehen

5 Homophone: Gleichlautende Wörter mit unterschiedlicher Schreibung und Bedeutung

Übung 4.2 Lies den Satz und entscheide:

there, their* oder *they're

1. Where are your books? __________ on my bed.

2. The children took __________ dog for a walk on Monday.

3. __________ is a big fish in the pond.

4. The girls are playing with __________ dolls.

5. Where are the dogs? __________ in the garden.

6. __________ father is a fireman.

7. Have you seen my bag? - Yes, it's over __________ .

8. Mandy and Tom are waiting for __________ mother to come home.

9. We went to Paris and stayed __________ for two weeks.

10. They have forgotten to put away __________ toys.

bed Bett
take took taken nehmen
for a walk zum Spazieren
pond See
doll Puppe

fireman Feuerwehrmann
bag Tasche
wait for warten auf
go went gone
stay bleiben

foget forgot fogotten vergessen
put away weglegen
toy Spiolzoug

Übung 4.3 Lies den Satz und entscheide:

***there, their* oder *they're*.**

1. __________ are cats running outside.

2. Suddenly __________ was a loud bang.

3. Jf anyone calls, ask for __________ number.

4. __________ goes the train.

5. Where is the ball? Oh, it is __________ .

6. __________ being served.

7. __________ you are. Your mother has been looking for you everywhere.

8. J don't know where __________ going.

9. __________ was once a little girl who was very poor.

10. __________ reading books.

suddenly plötzlich

call anrufen

ask fragen

be served serviert werden

look for suchen nach

read lesen

4.b) Homophone: *your* oder *you're*

Übung 4.4 Lies den Satz und entscheide:

your* oder *you're

1. This is _______ book.

2. He's from Chester and _______ from Bristol.

3. Are these _______ pencils?

4. Did you see _______ sister yesterday evening?

5. _______ a student.

6. _______ teacher is ill.

7. _______ walking home now.

8. _______ the winner.

9. _______ a star.

10. What do you think about _______ future?

yesterday gestern
evening Abend
teacher Lehrer
walk spazieren
winner Gewinner
think denken
future Zukunft

4.c) Homophone: *it's* oder *its*

Übung 4.5 Lies den Satz und entscheide:

it's*[6] oder *its

1. What's the time? ______ ten past twelve.

2. Put the CD in ______ place, please.

3. My hometown is famous for ______ old buildings.

4. J can't find my budgie, J think ______ flown away.

5. Peter, ______ never too late to learn how to play the piano.

6. The wolf made ______ way close to our house.

7. ______ been raining for five hours.

8. J'm interested in Denmark and ______ people.

9. J think ______ nice to have a dog.

10. Look at the horse! ______ hurt______ hoof.

put in place anbringen, einsetzen
famous berühmt
building Gebäude
budgie Wellensittich
think denken
fly flew flown fliegen
too late zu spät
how wie
make way seinen Weg gehen
close nahe
rain regnen
interested in interessiert an
hurt hurt hurt verletzen
hoof Hufe

---

6 *it's = it is oder it has*

Lösungsteil

Lösung zu Übung 1.1

1. smaller	smallest
2. greater	greatest
3. cooler	coolest
4. clearer	clearest
5. taller	tallest
6. newer	newest
7. older	oldest
8. sadder	saddest
9. bigger	biggest
10. hotter	hottest

Lösung zu Übung 1.2

1. cleverer	cleverest
2. simpler	simplest
3. nobler	noblest
4. gentler	gentlest
5. busier	busiest
6. dirtier	dirtiest
7. easier	easiest
8. prettier	prettiest
9. merrier	merriest
10. narrower	norrowest
11. sincerer	sincerest
12. preciser	precisest

Lösung zu Übung 1.3

1. beautiful	more beautiful	most beautiful
2. practical	more practical	most practical
3. important	more important	most important
4. remarkable	more remarkable	most remarkable
5. agreeable	more agreeable	most agreeable
6. pleasant	more pleasant	most pleasant
7. famous	more famous	most famous
8. precious	more precious	most precious

Lösung zu Übung 1.4

Roman. Steigerung	**Ausnahmen**	**Germ. Steigerun**
practical	good, better, best	richer, richest
usual	many, more, most	shorter, shortest
expensive	much, more, most	happier, happiest
remarkable	bad, worse, worst	merrier, merriest
pleasant	little, less, least	finer, finest
agreeable	ill, worse, worst	narrower, narrowest
beautiful		longer, longest
wonderful		older, oldest
curious		younger, youngest
famous		hotter, hottest
delicate		larger, largest
precious		colder, coldest
interesting		warmer, warmest
		cheaper, cheapest
	Germ. Steigerung >	quicker, quickest
	tinier, tiniest	darker, darkest
	politer, politest	nobler, noblest
	slower, slowest	gentler, gentlest
	easier, easiest	thinner, thinnest
	smaller, smallest	heavier, heaviest

Lösung für Übung 1.5

1. as small as a mouse
2. as sweet as sugar
3. as blue as the sky
4. as green as grass
5. as white as snow
6. as red as roses
7. as yellow as the sun
8. as stupid as a sheep
9. as black as the night
10. as hot as pepper
11. as soft as butter
12. as hard as stone

Lösung für Übung 1.6

1. Hamburg is larger than Hanover; Berlin is the biggest city in Germany.
2. Her hair is darker than his; she has the darkest hair.
3. This story is more exciting than hers; Peter's story is the most exciting one.
4. Tina is cleverer than her sister; Katie is the cleverest.
5. This task is harder than the other; that task is the hardest.
6. A Mercedes is more expensive than a Fiat; the Rolls-Royce is the most expensive car.
7. Silver is more precious than copper; gold is the most precious metal.
8. On Monday the weather was worse than yesterday; the day before yesterday was the worst day of this week.
9. The movie we saw on Sunday was more thrilling than the one we saw last week; on Friday we saw the most thrilling movie.
10. His idea is better than mine; yours is the best.

Lösung für Übung 1.7

1. He has less money than J have thought; he has spent the most.
2. Ron has made more mistakes than Luis; William has made the most mistakes.
3. This jacket is of fine/finer quality; we usually buy the finest quality.
4. The less you have to do with it the better it will be.
5. The results of this game were worse than those of last year. The results of two years ago were the worst.
6. My friend is older than your elder/eldest brother.
7. J will take the nearest way to the next bus stop.
8. Go straight on, at the next main street you turn left; that is the nearest way to the museum.
9. Please send me the latest edition of the magazine.
10. The last student to leave the hall must close the door.

Lösung zu Übung 1.8

1. The green car is as slow as the yellow car.
2. Linn is not as tall as Frida.
3. The trumpet is not as low as the tuba.
4. This copy is as weak as the other one.
5. Pete is as funny as Carl.
6. Today it's not as rainy as yesterday.
7. The banana dessert was as tasty as the strawberry dessert.
8. Grapefruit juice is not as sweet as lemonade.
9. Jill is as brave as Jamie.
10. Aluminium is not as heavy as iron.

Lösung zu Übung 1.9

1. Our kitchen is larger than the bedroom.
2. The bedroom is as large as the kid's room.
3. The drink tastes like strawberry smoothy.
4. The more people have, the more they want.
5. This offer is better than the other one.
6. Mr. King's offer is not so good as the one of Mr Flynn.
7. Jt doesn't look like that.
8. The drink was more tasty than we had expected.
9. The prices for cell phones are not so cheap as we have thought.
10. They behaved like true gentlemen.

Lösung zu Übung 1.10

1. The more you'll do sports, the better it will be for you.
2. German cars were more attractive than those of English companies.
3. French products are as good as English ones.
4. My friend's class-exercise is not so bad as Tom's.
5. She sings like a nightingale.
6. My elder sister is taller than my girl-friend.
7. Bikes are not as expensive as e-bikes.
8. People who do sports are often healthier than lazy people.
9. He is not so old as his cousin.
10. The more you know, the more you will be respected.

Lösung zu Übung 2.1

1. politely
2. richly
3. wonderfully
4. carefully
5. politically
6. electronically
7. slowly
8. quickly
9. unfortunately
10. surprisingly
11. decidedly
12. unexpectedly

Lösung zu Übung 2.2

1. terribly
2. remarkably
3. possibly
4. thinkably
5. truly
6. duly
7. wholy
8. easily
9. happily
10. fully

Lösung zu Übung 2.3

1. She reads a book quickly.
2. Lucy is a pretty girl.
3. The class is terribly loud today.
4. Luke is a good singer.
5. You can open this box easily.
6. Jt's a sunny day today.
7. She sings the song well.
8. He is a careful driver.
9. He drives the car carefully.
10. The cat cries loudly.

Lösung zu Übung 2.4

1. wonderfully	more wonderfully	most wonderfully
2. promptly	more promptly	most promptly
3. carefully	more carefully	most carefully
4. beautifully	more beautifully	most beautifully
5. horribly	more horribly	most horribly
6. dangerously	more dangerously	most dangerously
7. soon	sooner	soonest
8. late	later	latest
9. early	earlier	earliest
10. friendly	friendlier	friendliest
11. fast	faster	fastest
12. high	higher	highest

Lösung zu Übung 2.5

1. you never go
2. he often flies
3. she usually plays
4. it often goes
5. we never go
6. you sometimes go
7. they often fly
8. she usually does
9. it sometimes plays
10. he never goes
11. they usually sit
12. we often go
13. you usually play
14. he often flies
15. J sometimes sit

Lösung zu Übung 2.6

1. She <u>often</u> listens to the music.
2. He <u>sometimes</u> reads the newspapers.
3. Nick is <u>never</u> sad.
4. Sam <u>usually</u> looks very happy.
5. J <u>sometimes</u> have milk for breakfast.
6. Luca and Finn are <u>often</u> ill.
7. Jane <u>usually</u> helps her father washing the car.
8. They <u>never</u> watch TV in the afternoon.
9. Kenny <u>never</u> drinks Coke.

Lösung zu Übung 2.7

1. J ran on Monday.
2. You went last year.
3. He flew last month.
4. She played in the team in 2010.
5. Jt was one year ago.
6. We didn't go two years ago.
7. He didn't go to Paris last month.
8. They didn't fly on Friday.

Lösung zu Übung 2.8

1. She played with the dog yesterday.
2. He went to Canady a year ago.
3. She sat in the train on Sunday.
4. We went to the cinema yesterday.
5. You didn't play cards yesterday, but PC games.
6. He went to Texas two years ago.
7. J wasn't at home yesterday.
8. She lived in England ten years ago.

Lösungen zu Übung 3.1

1. We need some apples.
2. You can't buy any teddy bears in this shop.
3. We haven't got any pears just now.
4. Peter has bought some new gloves.
5. She always takes some water with her coffee.
6. J have seen some beautiful mugs in this shop.
7. J have some books for you.
8. There are some glasses on the table.
9. Pam doesn't have any pens on her desk.
10. There aren't any sweets in my bag.

Lösungen zu Übung 3.2

1. Have you got any strawberries ?
2. There are some rubbers on the floor.
3. Did you get the flour ? No, they hadn't got any .
4. You should eat some healthy food.
5. We had to wait for some hours.
6. Js there any milk left ?
7. They didn't sing any songs J knew.
8. Here is some coffee, but there isn't any sugar.
9. J'm looking for some good advice.
10. There is no cheese in the fridge. Let's go and buy some.

Lösungen zu Übung 3.3

1. Can J have some of these blueberries?
2. We saw some fish in the sea.
3. They went to Paris without any money.
4. Buy 1kg of pears if you find some.
5. Would you like any more lemonade?
6. Come and see me any time you want.
7. She never does any work.
8. You can take any train to Munich.
9. John and Bill never give their mother any help.
10. There's hardly any butter left.

Lösungen zu Übung 3.4

1. J've got something in my ear.
2. There is someone at the door.
3. We haven't heard anything about John's trip to Paris. When will he tell us ?
4. Do you work anywhere near Coronation Street ?
5. Someone wants to see you.
6. Has anyone seen my little sister ?
7. My mother asked me something.
8. Can J have anything to drink ?
9. Don't worry. Someone can tell you the way to the town center.
10. J don't know anything about it.
11. Do something about it now !
12. Js anyone at the door ?

Lösungen zu Übung 4.1

1. The children are there.
2. They are there finally!
3. Can they stay there?
4. They walked there with Sandy.
5. They are not there yet.
6. There it is.
7. They all went there in Ron's bus.

Lösungen zu Übung 4.2

1. Where are your books? They're on my bed.
2. The children took their dog for a walk on Monday.
3. There is a big fish in the pond.
4. The girls are playing with their dolls.
5. Where are the dogs? They're in the garden.
6. Their father is a fireman.
7. Have you seen my bag? - Yes, it's over there.
8. Mandy and Tom are waiting for their mother to come home.
9. We went to Paris and stayed there for two weeks.
10. They have forgotten to put away their toys.

Lösungen zu Übung 4.3

1. There are cats running outside.
2. Suddenly there was a loud bang.
3. Jf anyone calls, ask for their number.
4. There goes the train.
5. Where is the ball? Oh, it is there.
6. They're being served.
7. There you are. Your mother has been looking for you everywhere.
8. J don't know where they're going.
9. There was once a little girl who was very poor.
10. They're reading books.

Lösungen zu Übung 4.4

1. This is your book.
2. He's from Chester and you're from Bristol.
3. Are these your pencils?
4. Did you see your sister yesterday evening?
5. You're a student.
6. Your teacher is ill.
7. You're walking home now.
8. You're the winner.
9. You're a star.
10. What do you think about your future?

Lösungen zu Übung 4.5

1. What's the time? Jt's ten past twelve.
2. Put the CD in its place, please.
3. My hometown is famous for its old buildings.
4. J can't find my budgie, J think it's flown away.
5. Peter, it's never too late to learn how to play the piano.
6. The wolf made its way close to our house.
7. Jt's been raining for five hours.
8. J'm interested in Denmark and its people.
9. J think it's nice to have a dog.
10. Look at the horse! Jt's hurt its hoof.